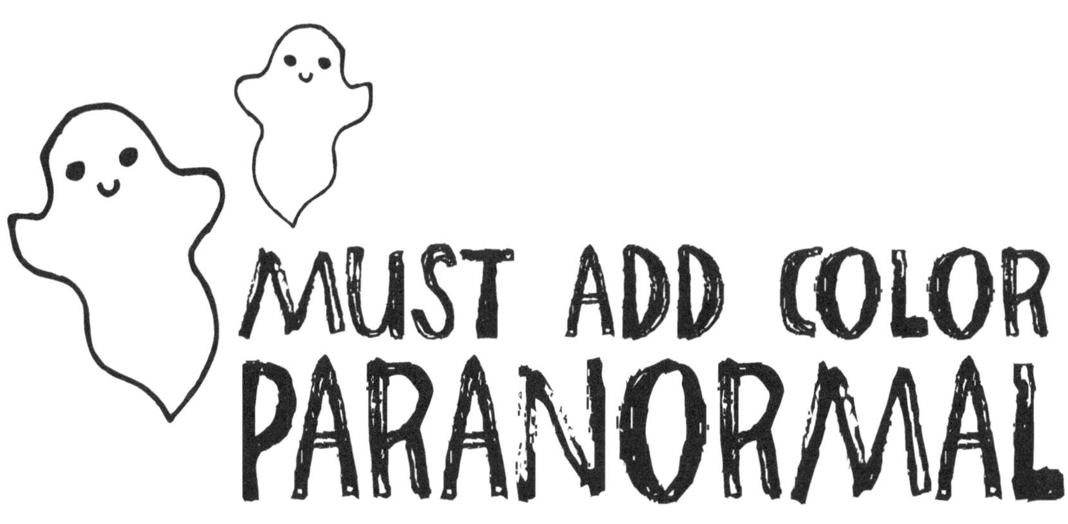

# MUST ADD COLOR PARANORMAL

by STEPH HARGROVE

Share your work!

#MUSTADDCOLORPARANORMAL
@ART4THEPPL



ISBN 978-1-533-13376-2

CROP CIRCLE

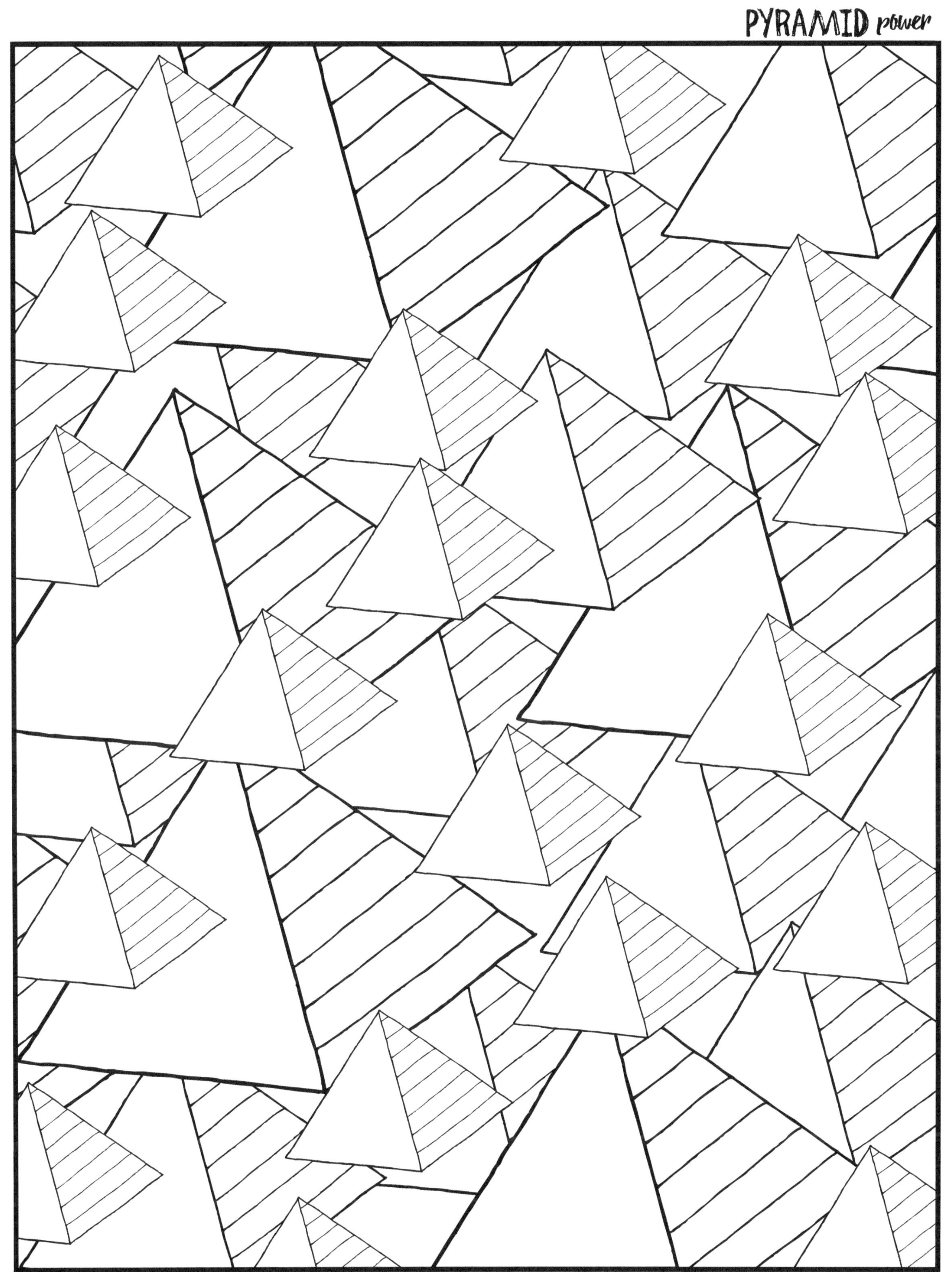
PYRAMID power

# NAZCA BIRD

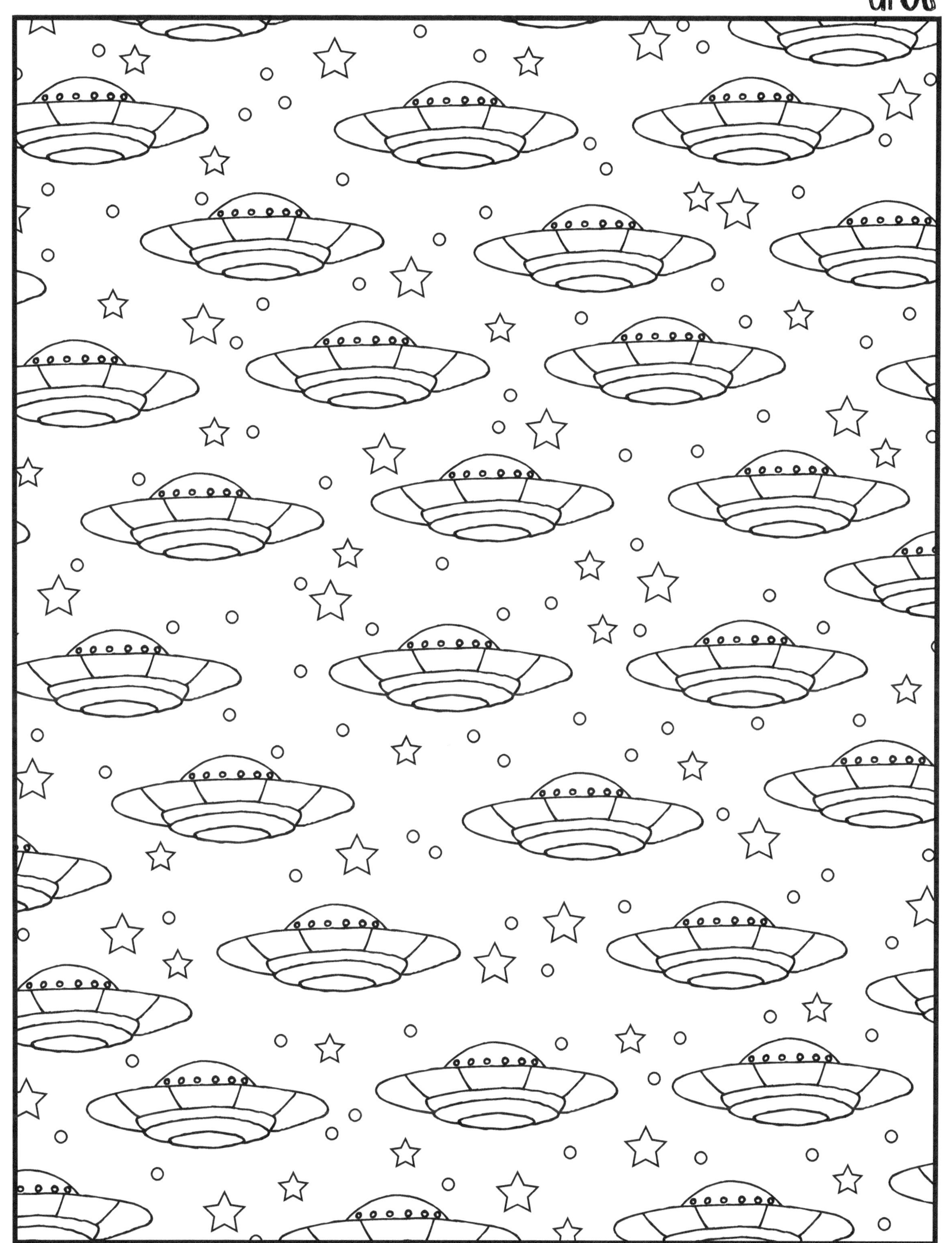

VORTEX

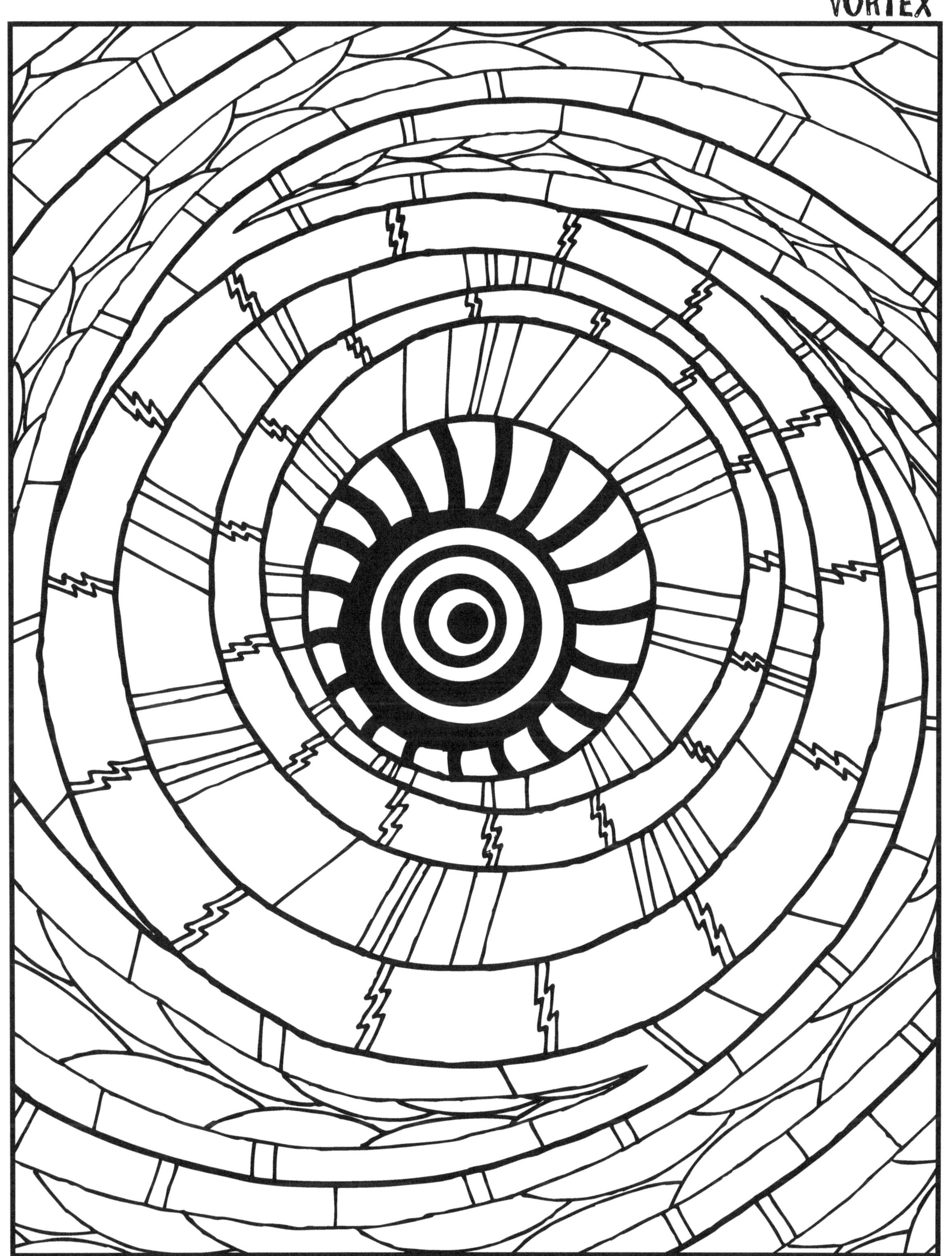

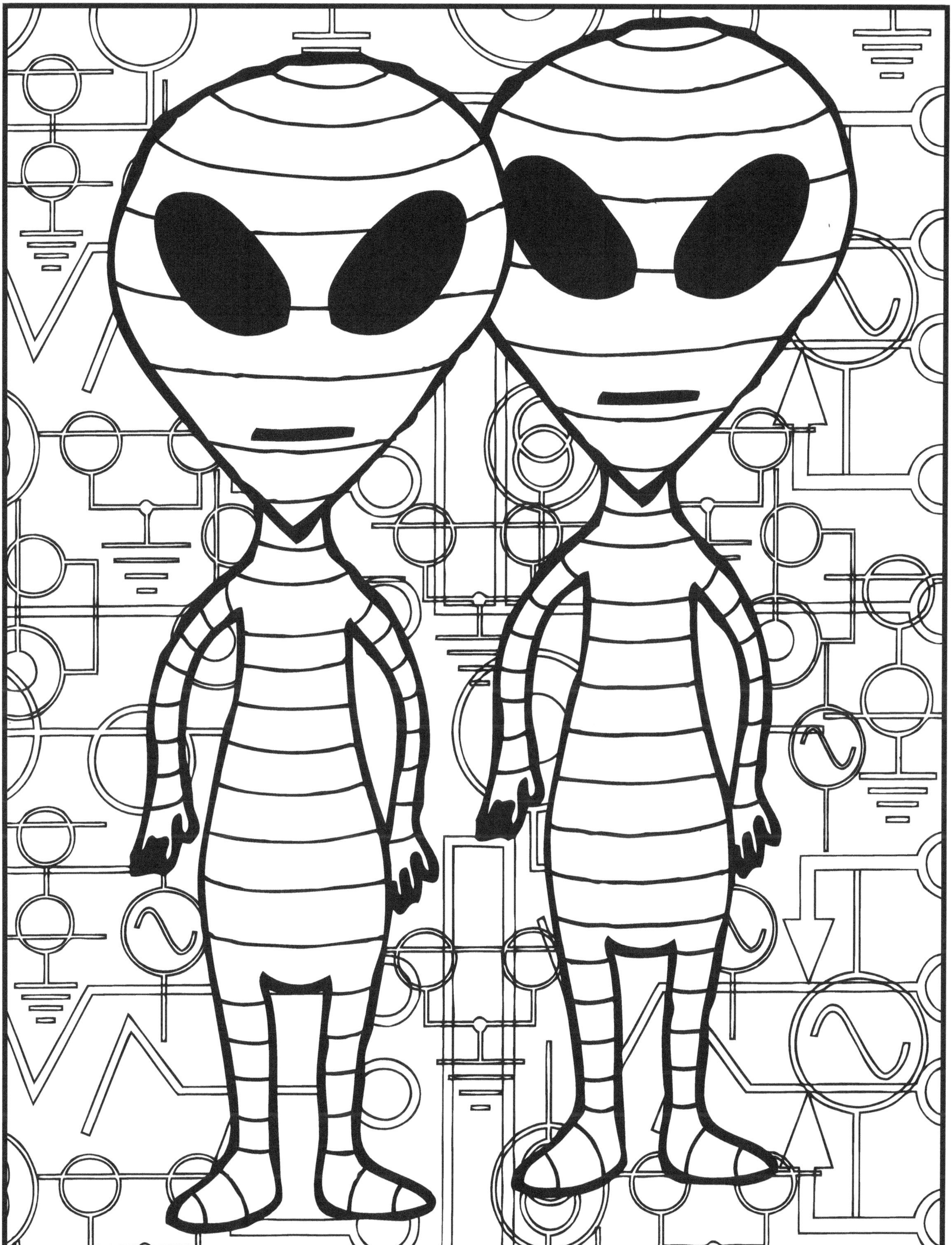

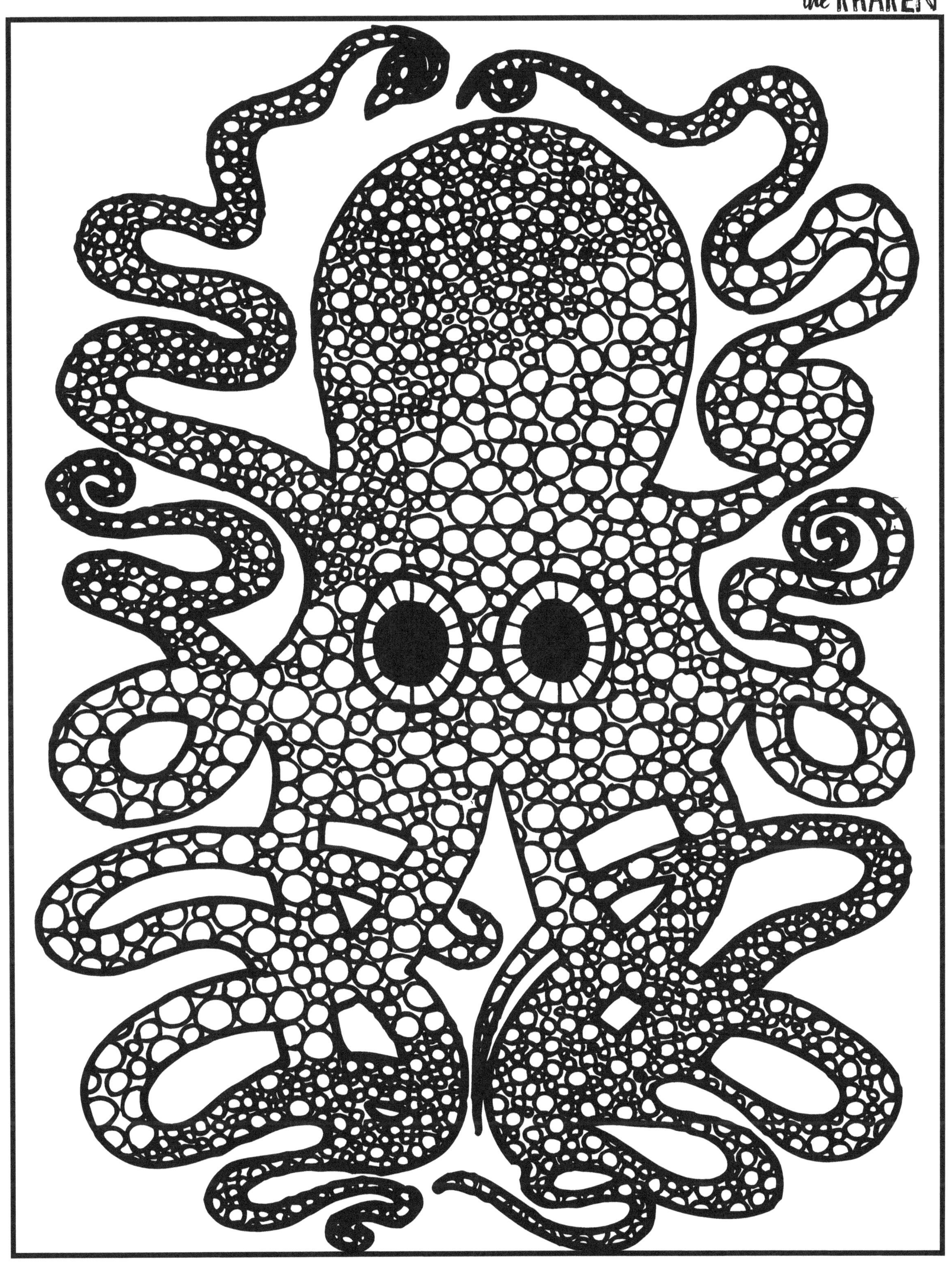

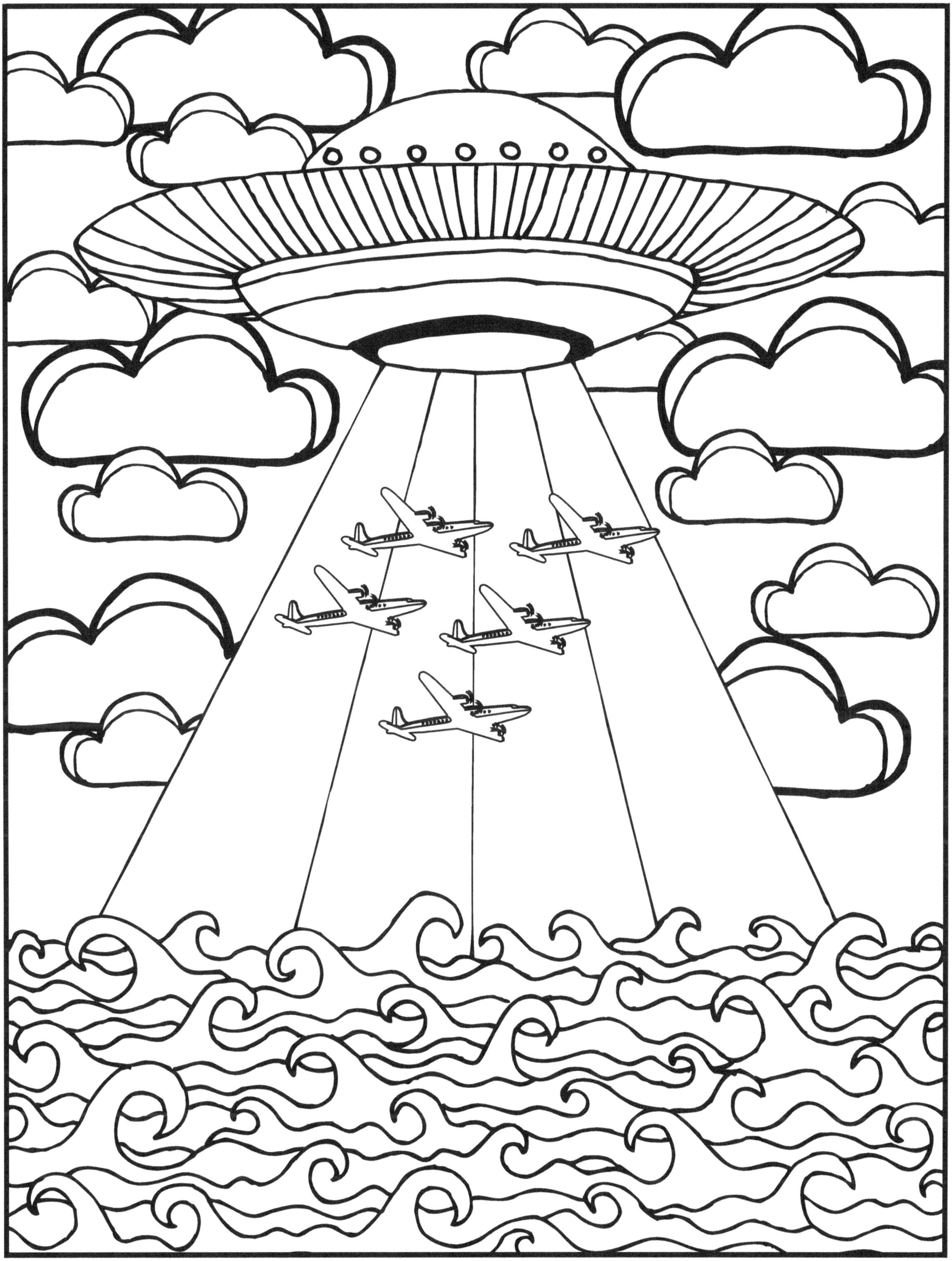

# BERMUDA TRIANGLE

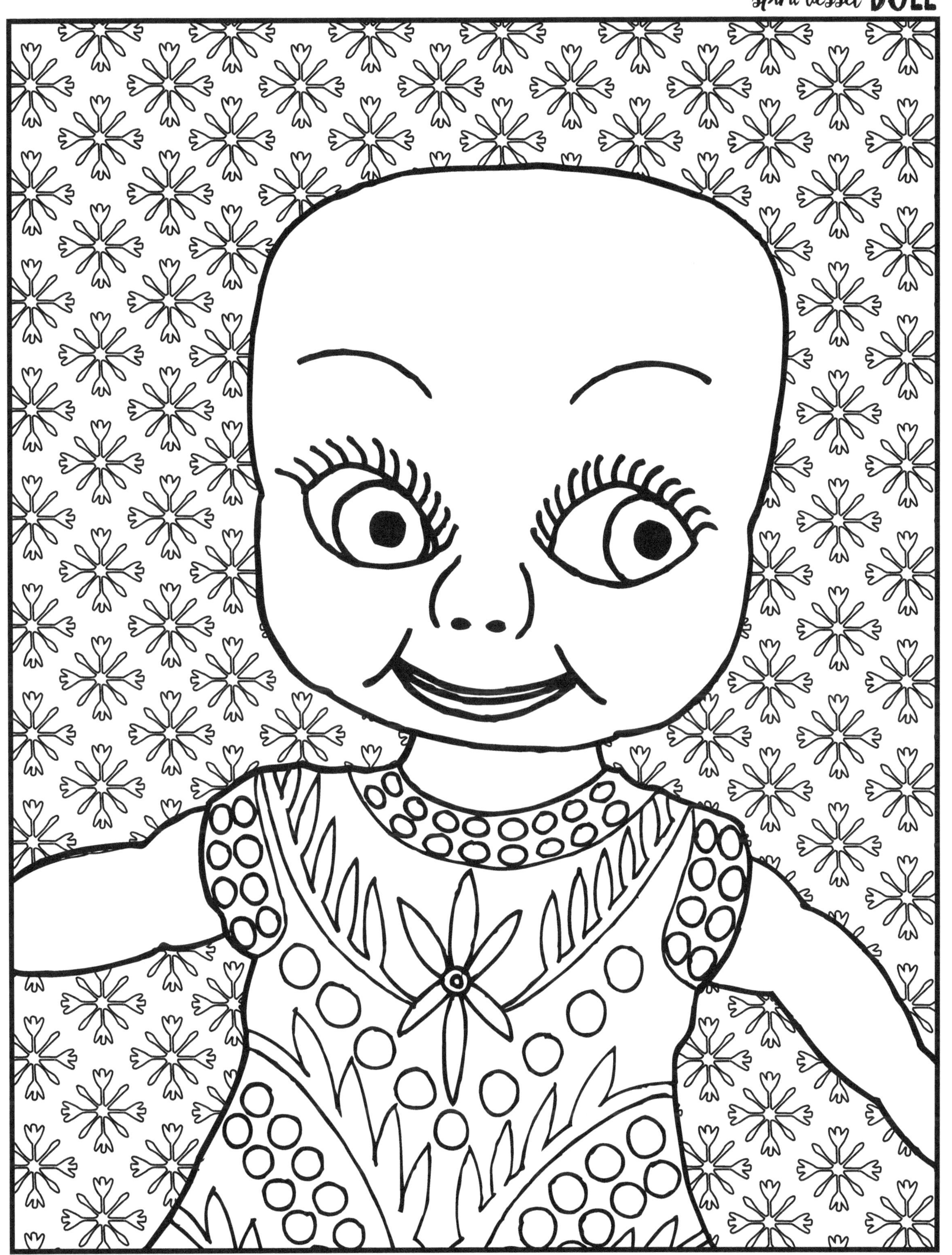

# ROSWELL ROCK

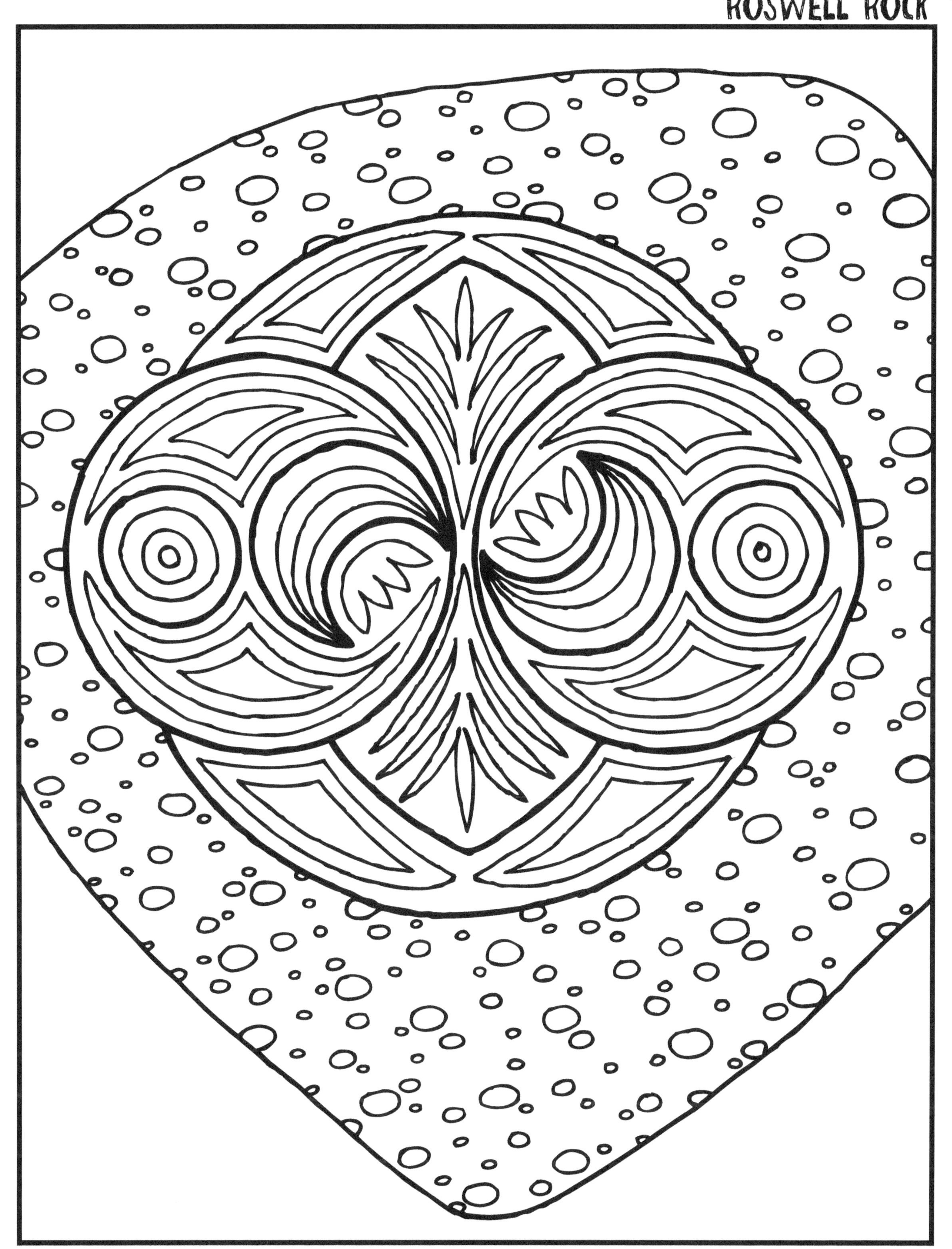

EVP

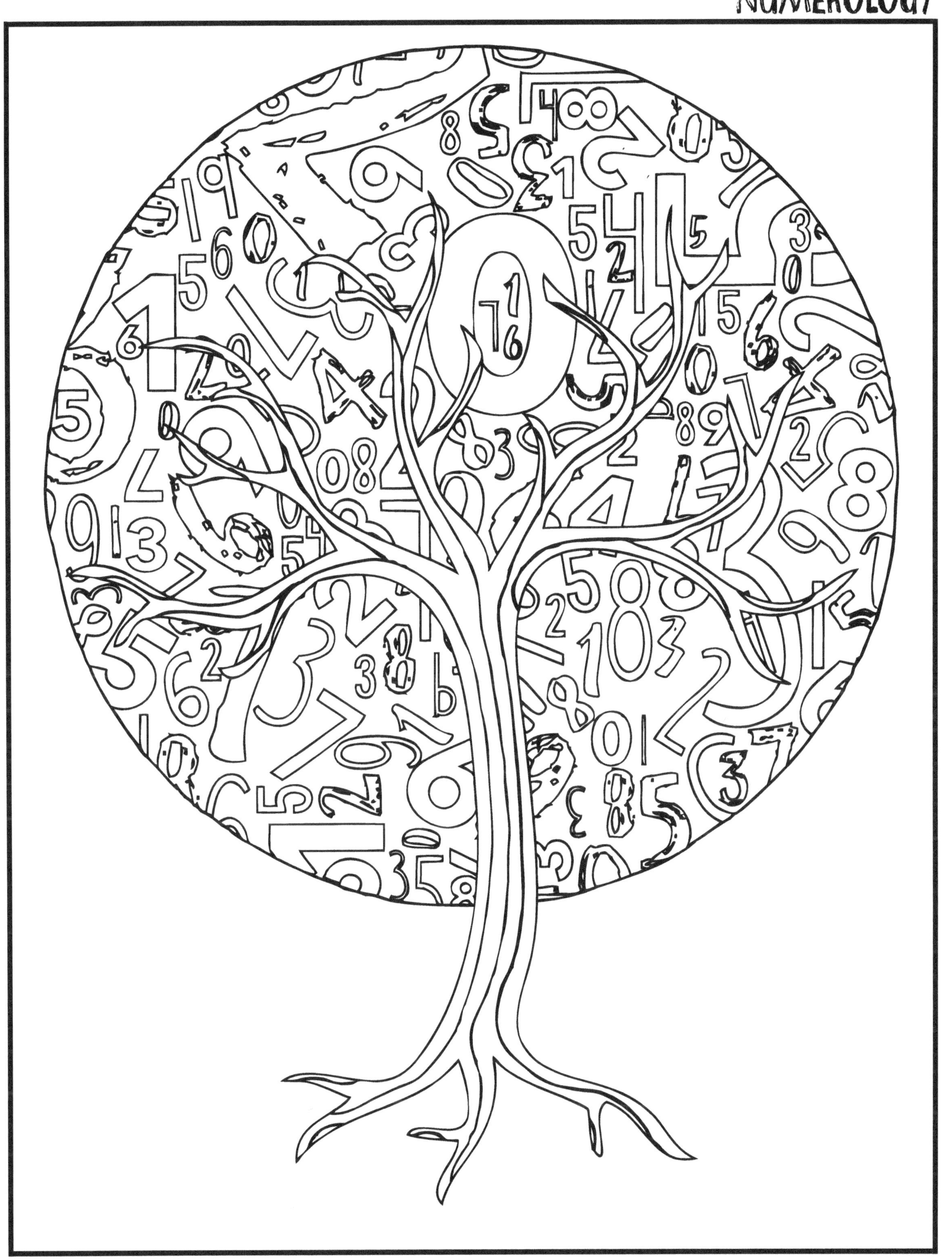

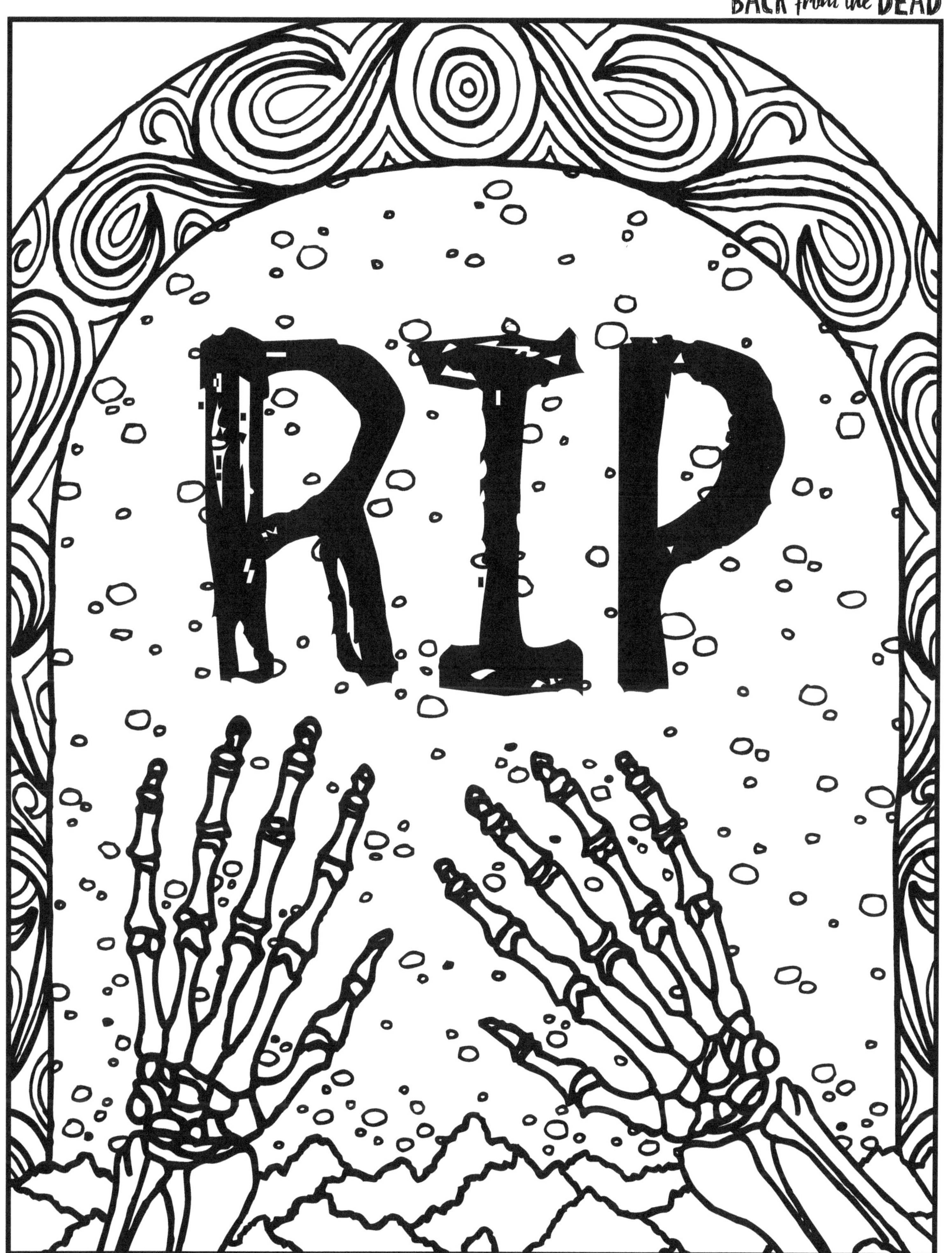
RIP

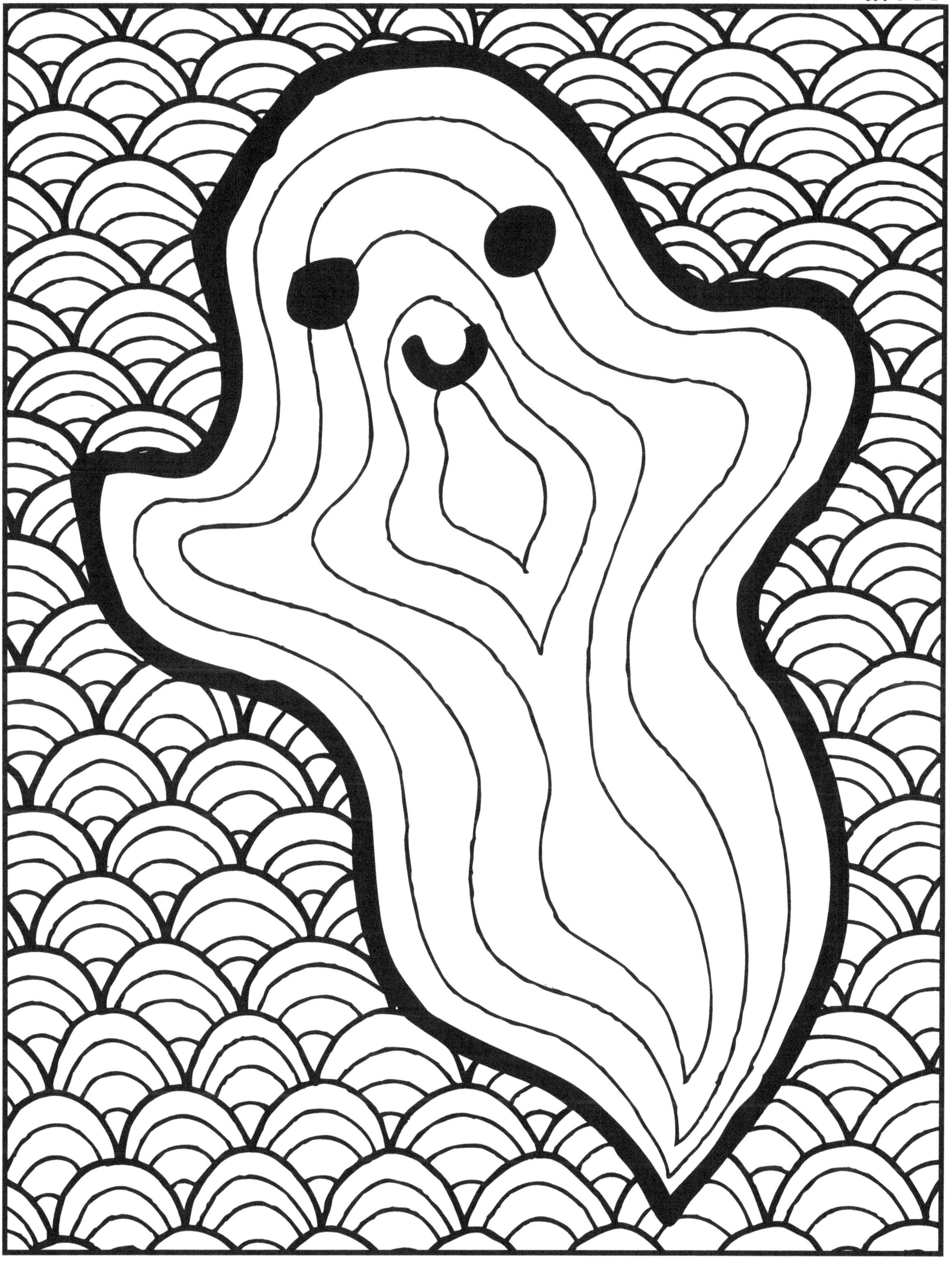

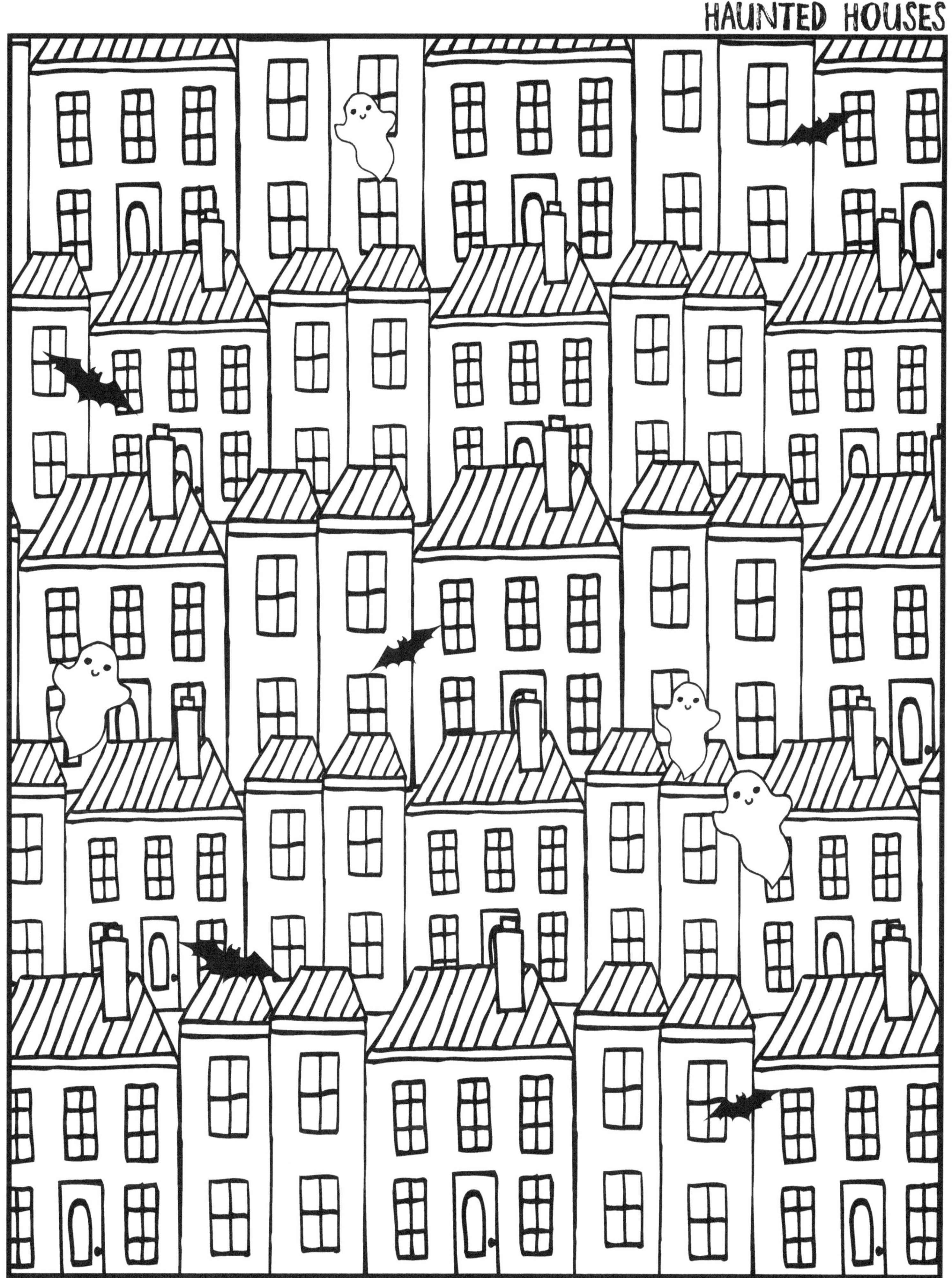

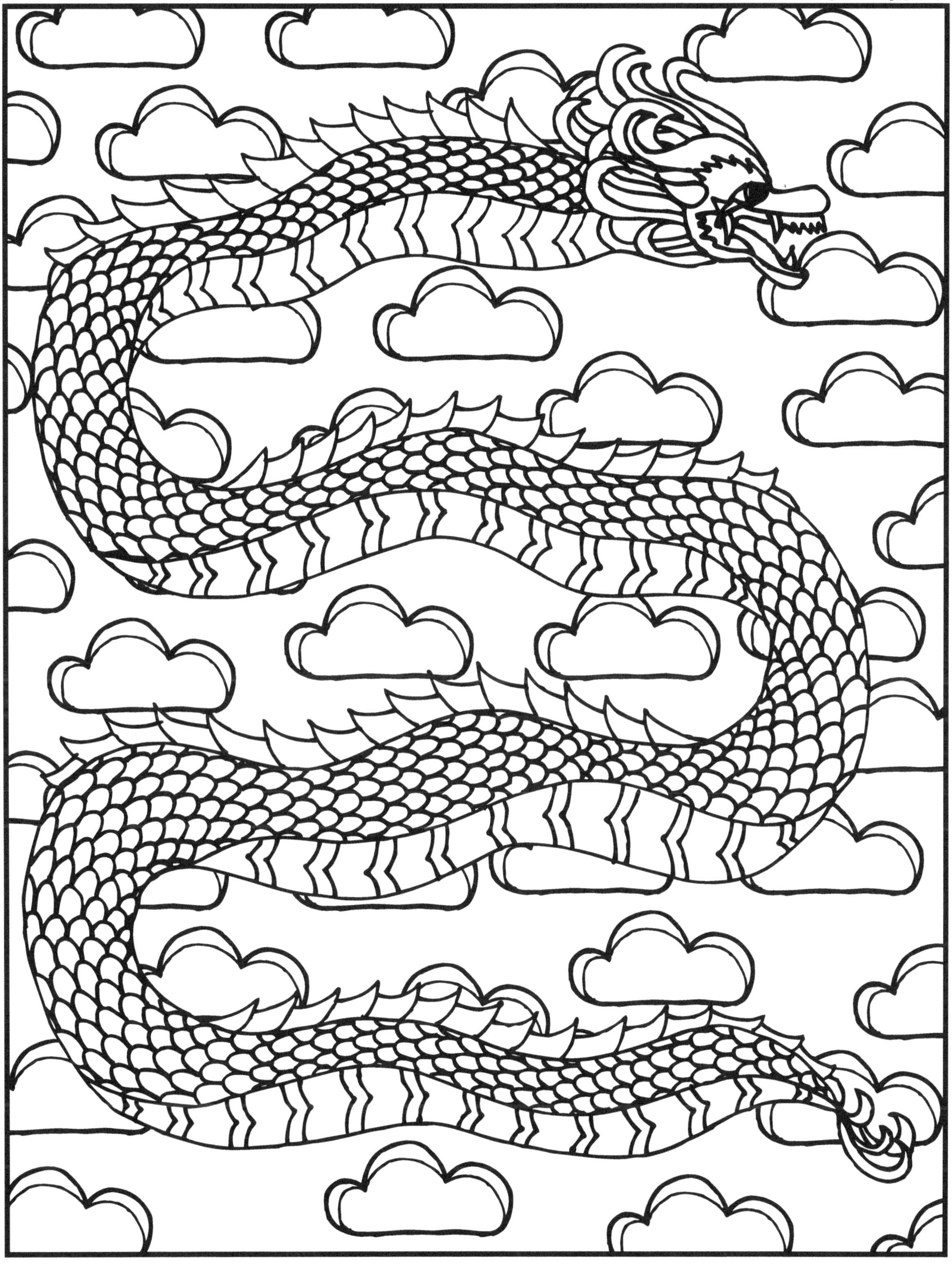

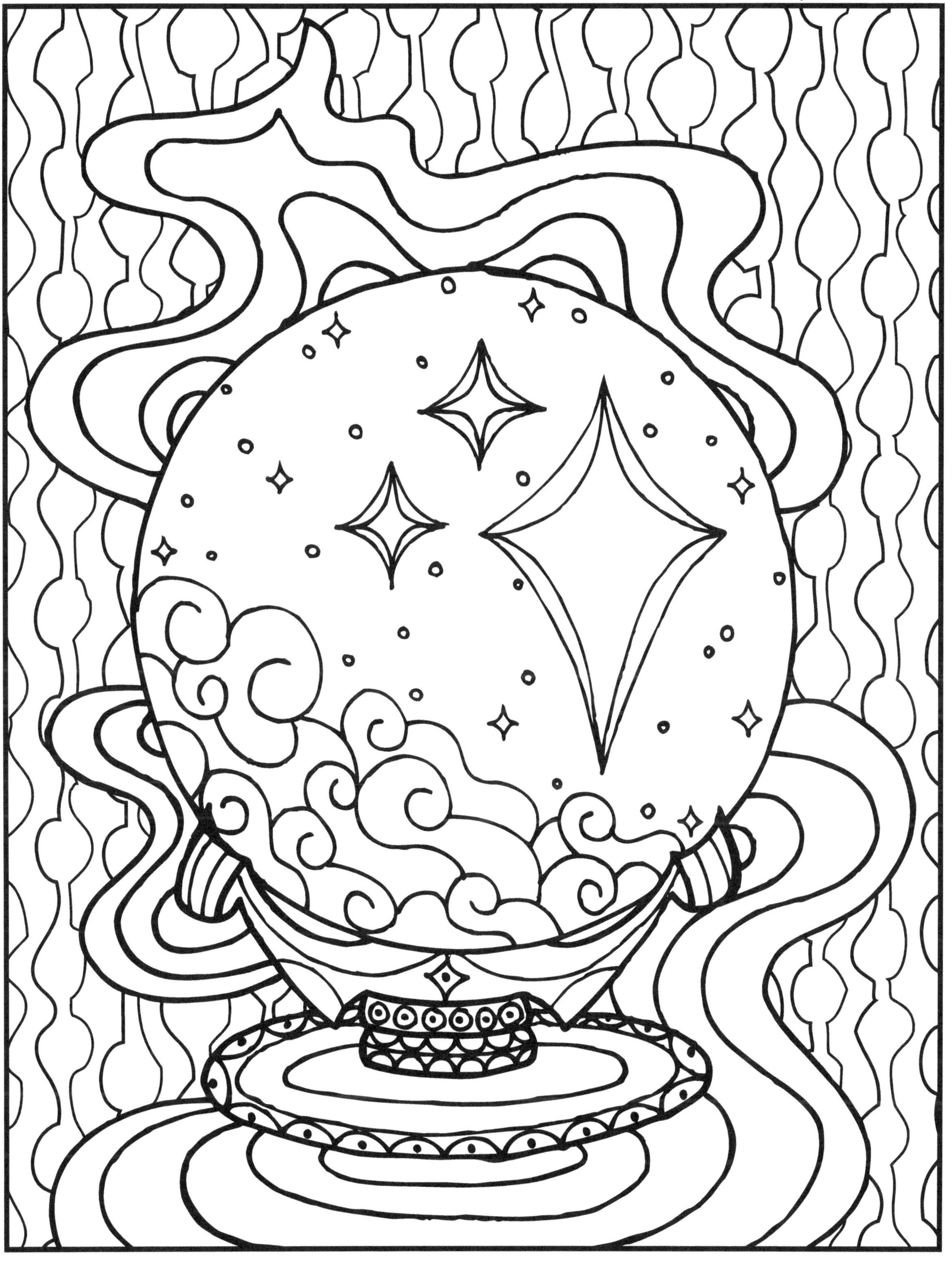

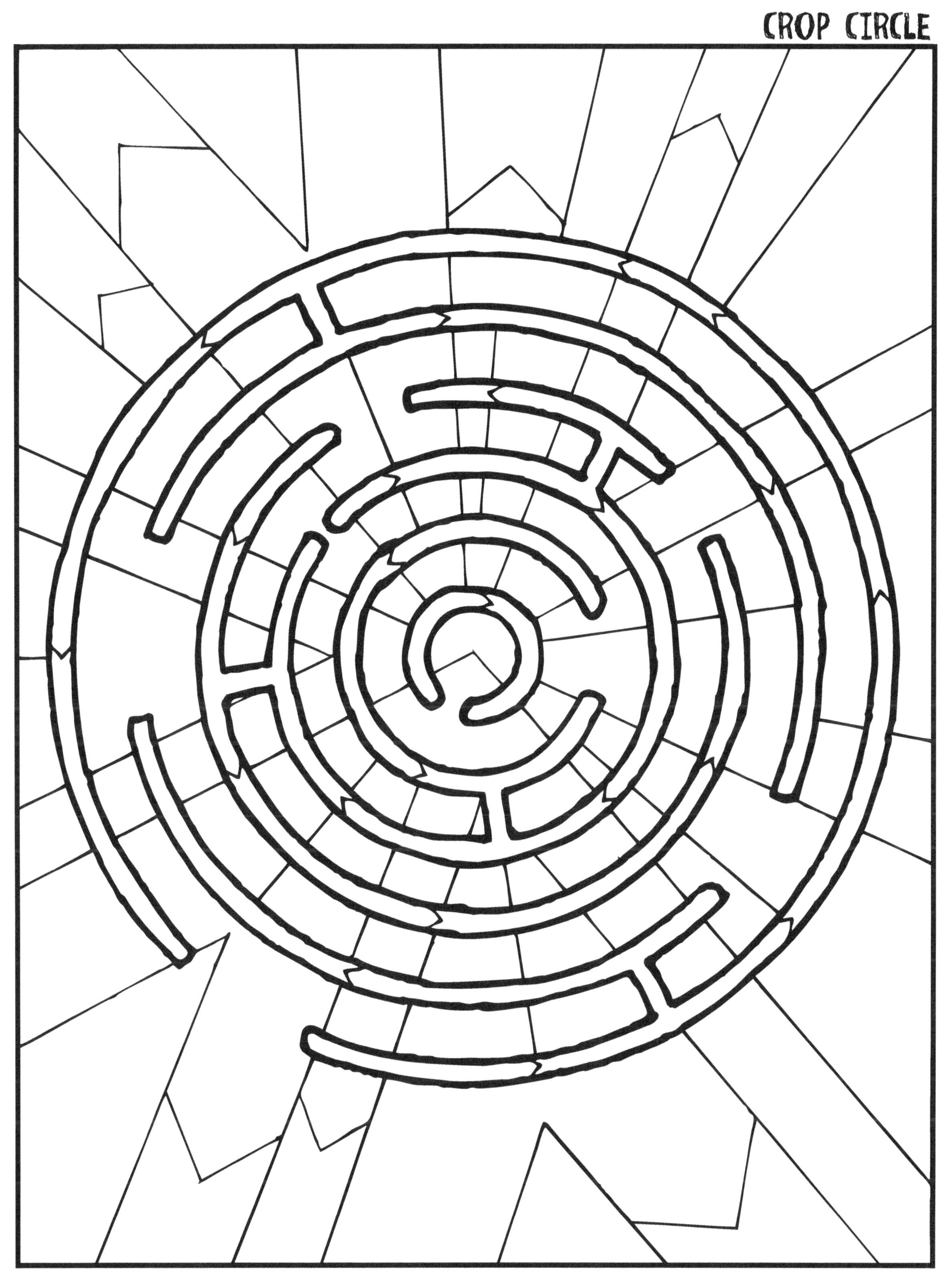

VOODOO DOLL

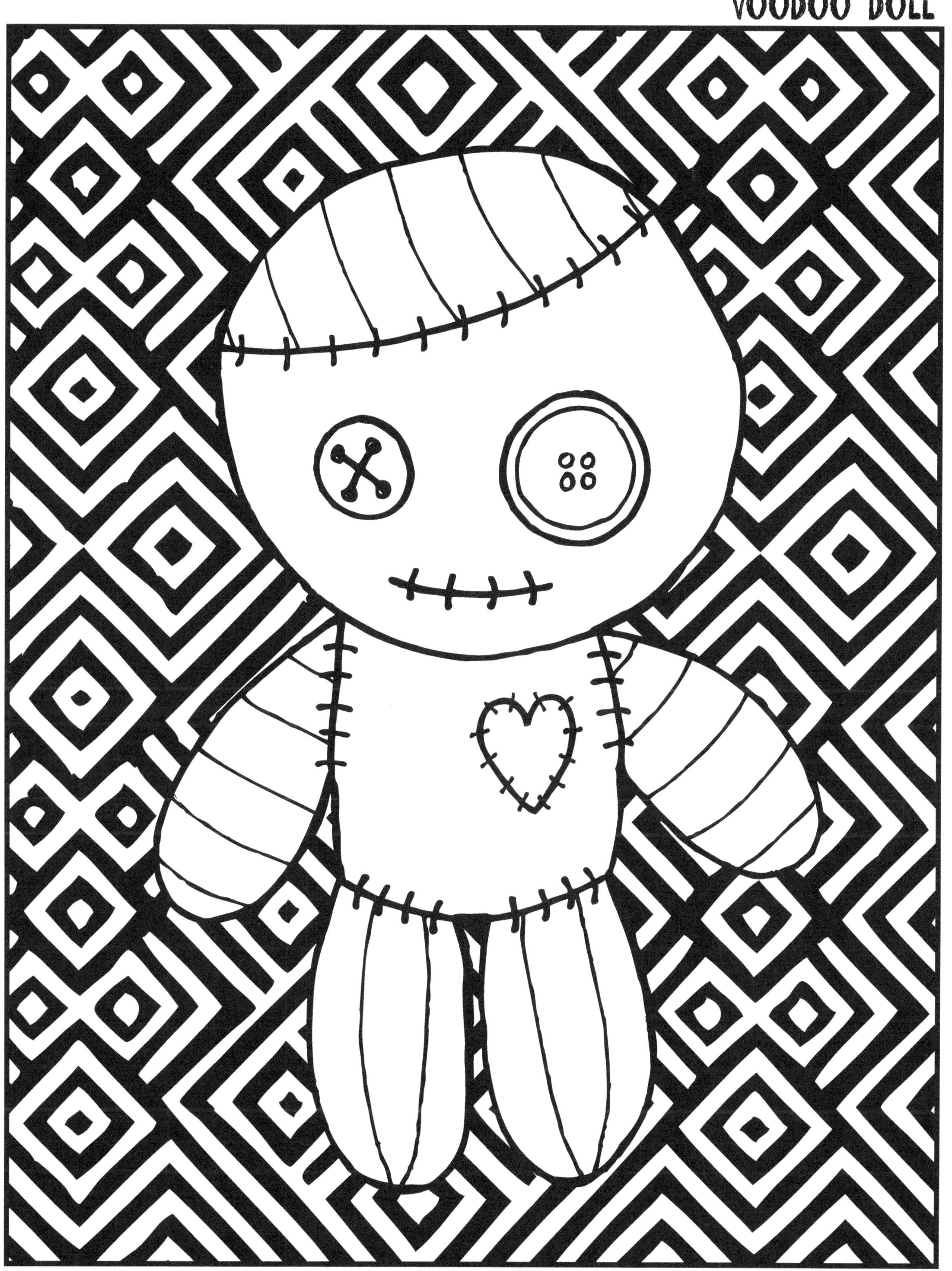

gray ALIENS

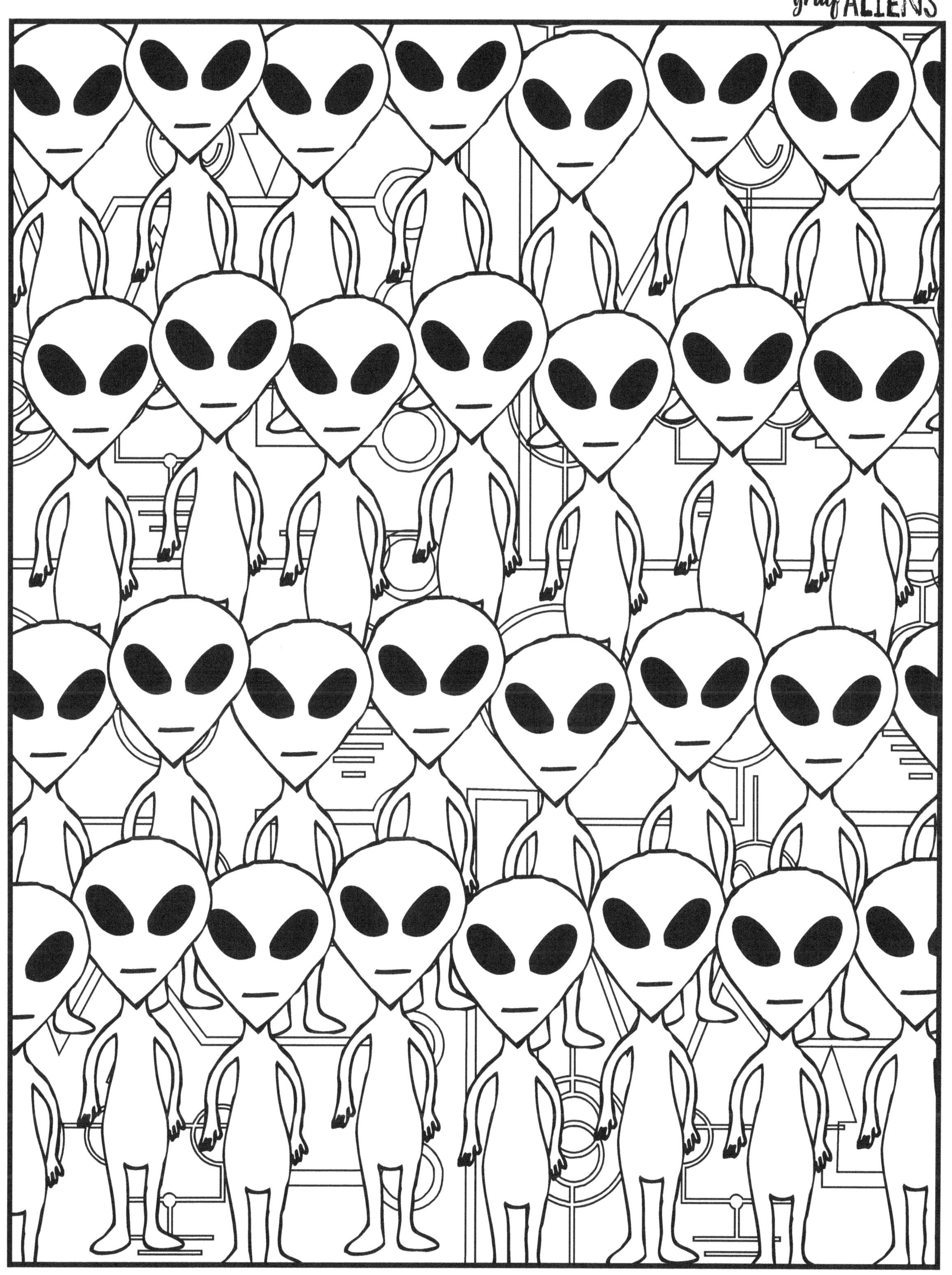

CRYSTAL SKULL

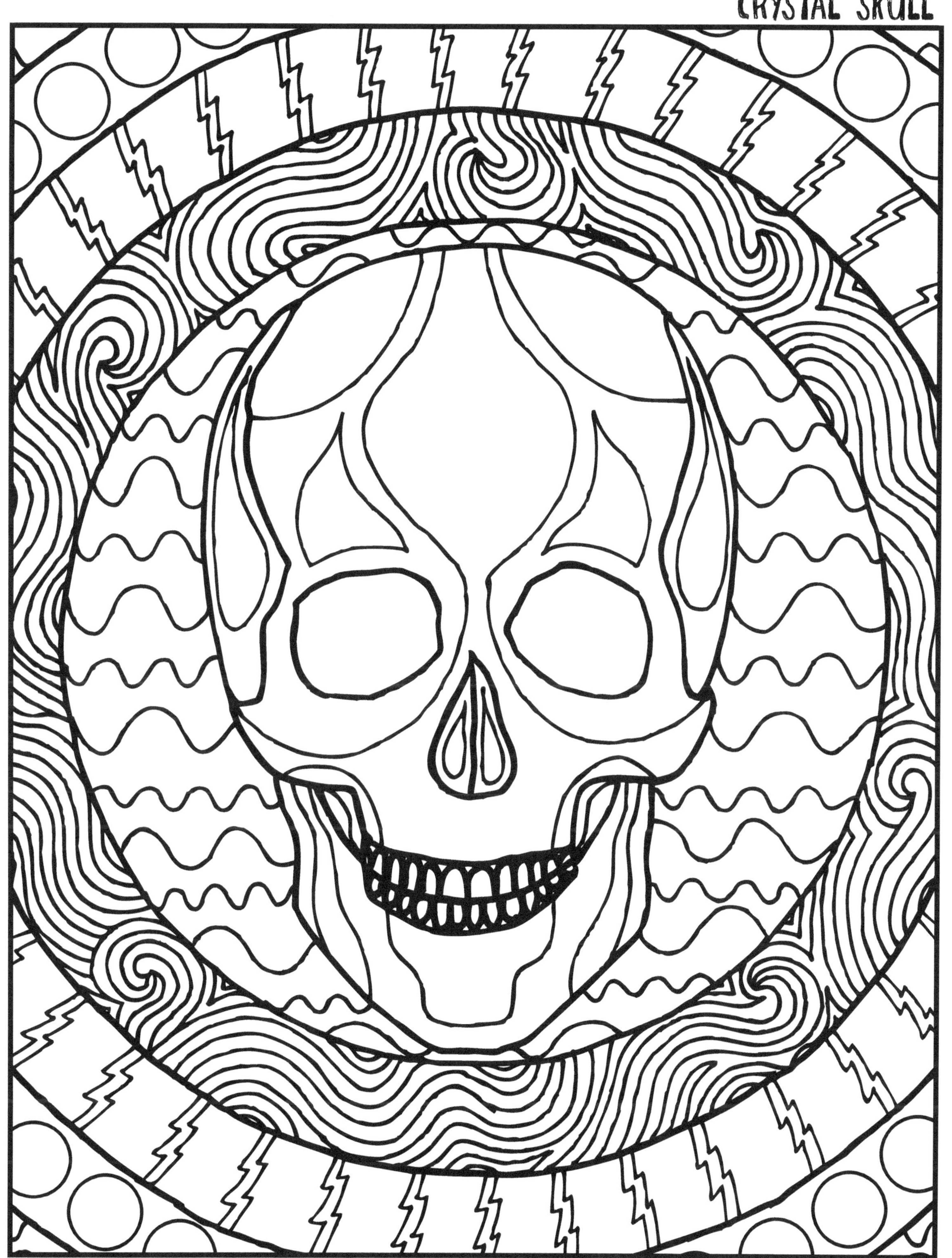

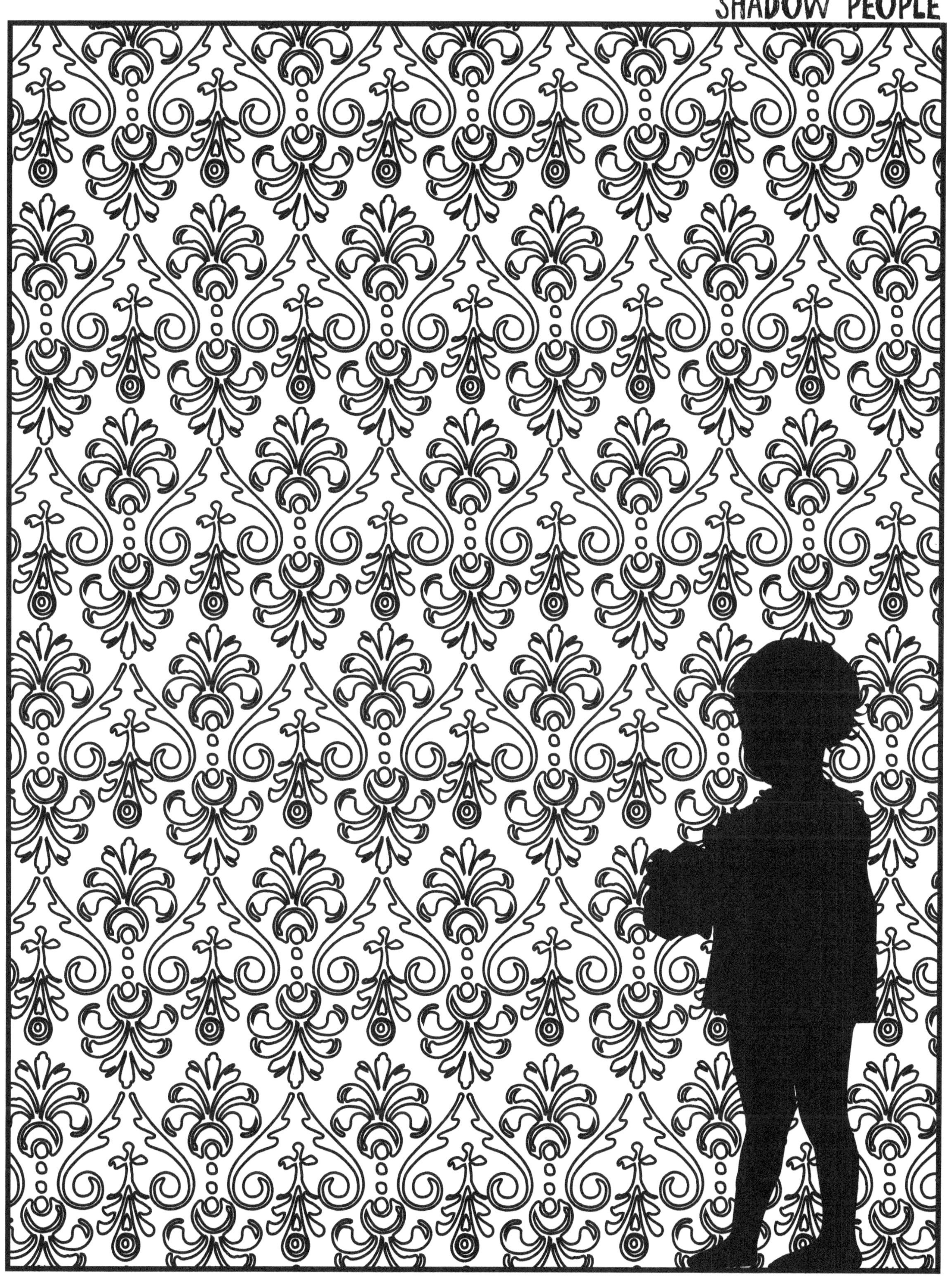

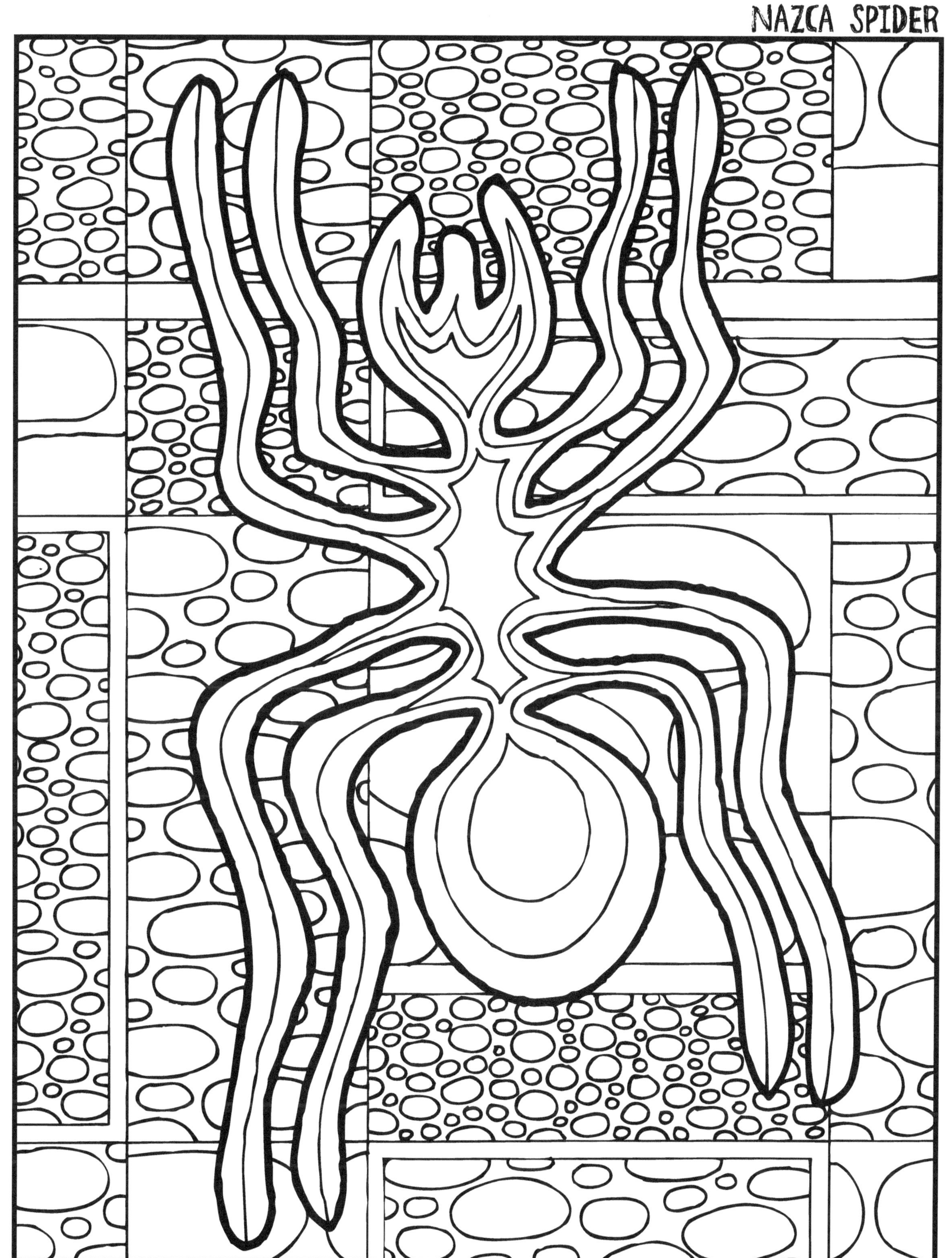
NAZCA SPIDER

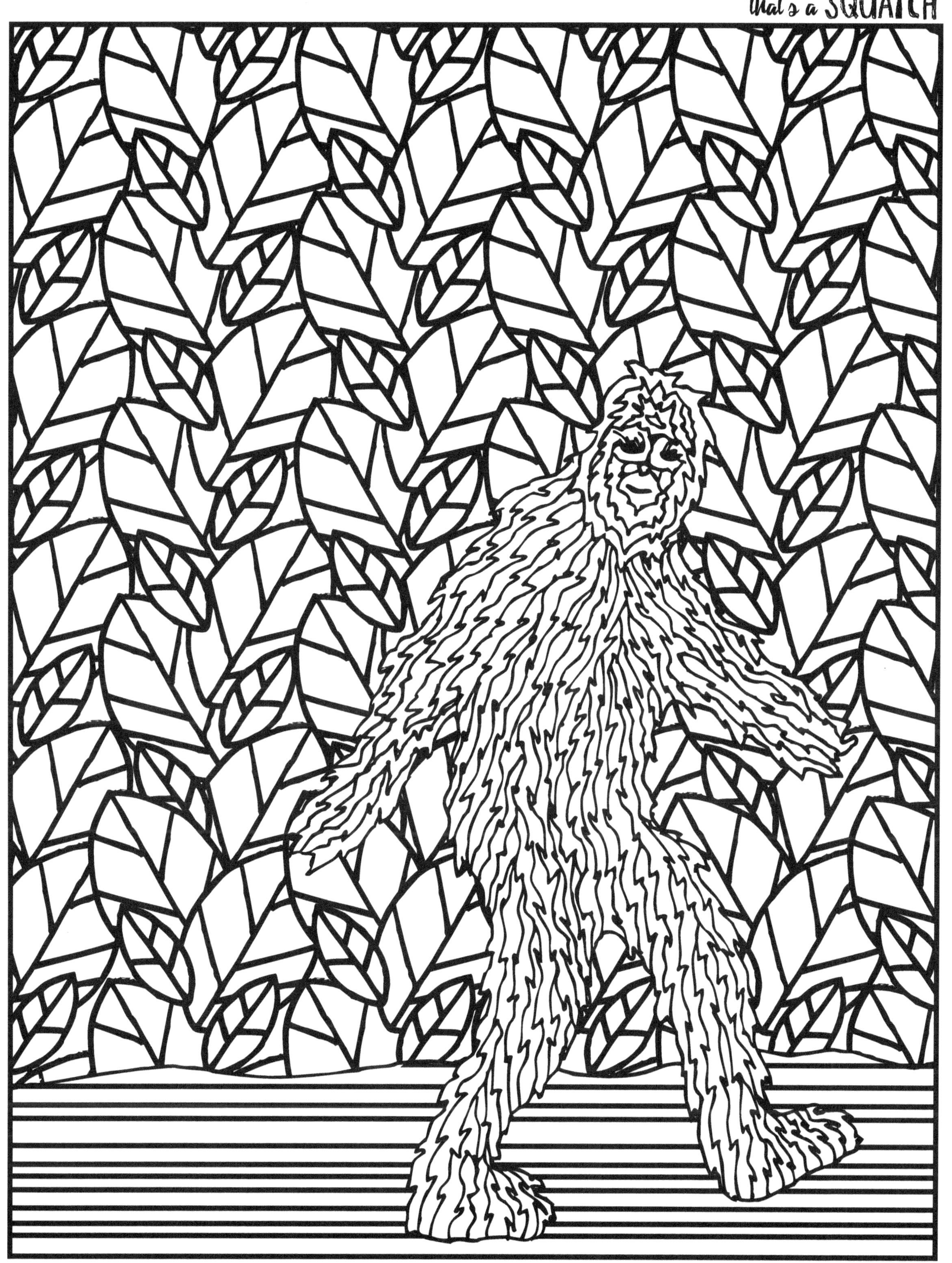

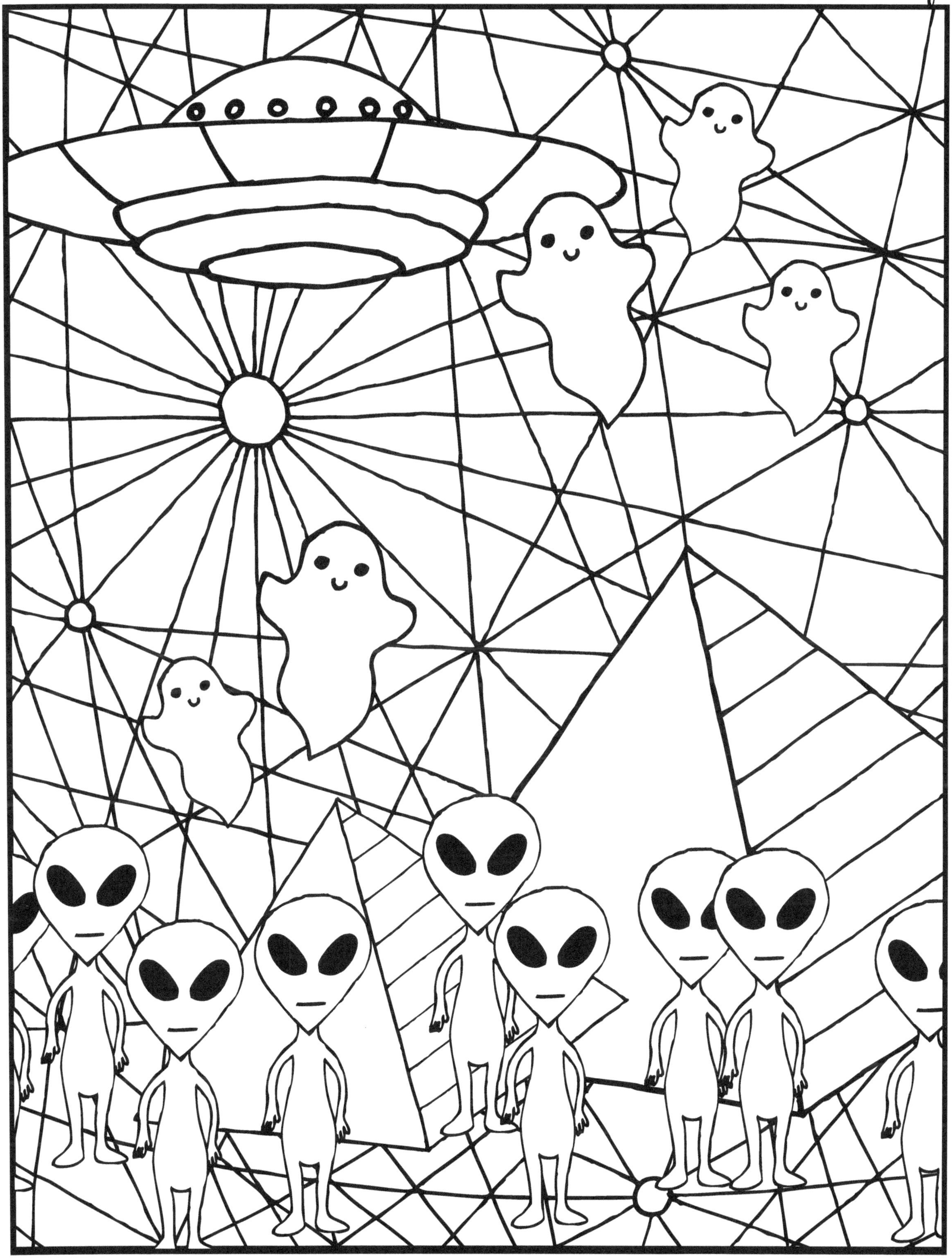

www.ingramcontent.com/pod-product-compliance
Lightning Source LLC
Chambersburg PA
CBHW080547190526
45169CB00007B/2675

* 9 7 8 1 5 3 3 1 3 3 7 6 2 *